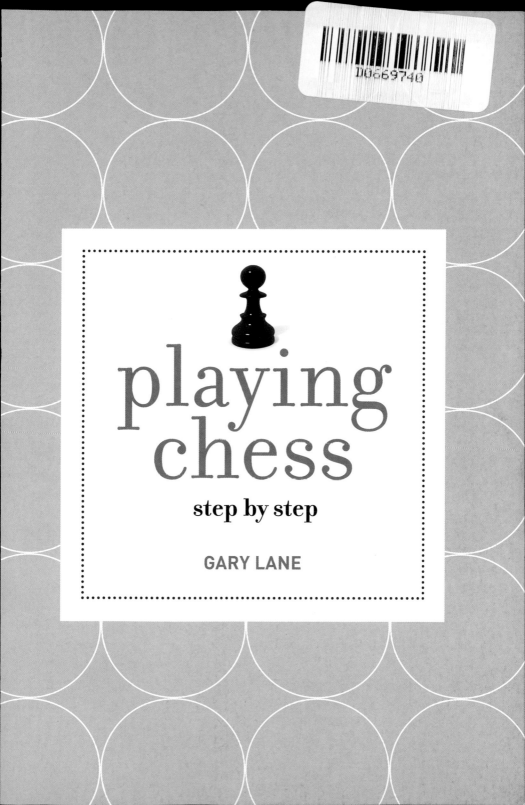

# playing chess

## step by step

### GARY LANE

Playing Chess:
Step by Step
by Gary Lane

**Mud Puddle Books**
NEW YORK

Published by
Mud Puddle Books
54 W. 21st Street
Suite 601
New York, NY 10010 USA
info@mudpuddlebooks.com

Hinkler Books Pty Ltd
45-55 Fairchild Street
Heatherton Victoria 3202
Australia
www.hinklerbooks.com

ISBN: 978-1-60311-091-4

Interior Design by Amy Trombat

Printed and bound in China

# CONTENTS

# ABOUT CHESS

Chess is a fun and easy game to learn, and can be played by people of all ages. It is a mind game played between two people; one person has white pieces and the other, black. Chess is also an excellent way of developing concentration skills.

Once played by royalty, chess is now learned and played by millions of people all around the world. It is even considered a sport in many countries. Beginners can soon become good enough to challenge experienced players, or even beat a computer.

## Anyone Can Play

Chess is a game with no physical or age barriers; a child of twelve will often be seen beating adults. It is the perfect game for the Internet, with thousands of people playing on computers every day, all around the world. It is not unusual to have a quick game with someone in the USA, then France, maybe England and finally, Australia.

## Winning Prizes

There are chess tournaments in just about every country of the world, where it is possible to win money or trophies. Some people think that only old men with beards play the game and win prizes, but this is not correct. The majority of players are young people.

## Sharpen Your Mental Skills

Playing chess is a fun and interesting way for players to sharpen their mental skills. Chess players learn problem solving skills and goal setting skills during the game. Chess also improves concentration, memory and patience. These important skills can then be used in other areas of life, such as when you are at school or work, or playing other sports.

## Why is Chess So Popular?

Chess is popular because it is an exciting game! You can play it at home or school, on a train or a plane, or outside, in a park. All you need is a chess board and pieces, or a computer.

Chess has never been completely mastered by anyone, with world champions often saying they have more to learn. The game offers a lifetime of fun and excitement for players of every standard. And one thing that everyone agrees on is that winning is enjoyable!

## FAMOUS PLAYERS

The game of chess has produced many famous players from around the world. In some countries, these players are treated almost like movie stars! Other chess players like to study their games and watch them play.

**Garry Kasparov** is one of the greatest chess players of all time. Born in Azerbaijan in 1963, he began playing chess at the age of four. By the time he was twelve he had become a champion player and was beating adults. In 1980, he won the chess Junior World Championship and became a Grandmaster of the game, at only seventeen!

Kasparov went on to become overall world champion in 1985 – a title he held until 2000. He is still rated the number one player of all time in the world.

**Judit Polgár** is the best female chess player in history. She was born in Hungary in 1976, and is part of the famous Polgár family of chess players. Her sisters, Sofia and Zsuzsa, are also brilliant players. Judit became a Grandmaster of the game at the age of fifteen.

Polgár has had great results against all of the world's best chess players, including a win against Garry Kasparov.

**Viswanathan ("Vishy") Anand** is one of the most exciting chess players in the world today. Born in India in 1969, he first began to play chess at the age of six. He became India's national chess champion at the age of sixteen and then, when he was eighteen, he won the World Junior Championship. He went on to win the World Championship in 2000, when he was thirty-one.

Anand used to play all his games very quickly. Once, he beat America's top player in the amazing time of ten minutes! However, he stopped his speedy style when he once made a big mistake and lost in six moves.

# HISTORY OF CHESS

Monopoly was invented in 1934 and Trivial Pursuit first appeared in 1981, but chess is known to be at least 1500 years old. It is first mentioned in a Persian (Iranian) story in the sixth century. It is similar to the Indian game "Chaturanga," which has pieces resembling an Indian army of chariots, cavalry, elephants and foot soldiers.

The game was introduced to Spain in the tenth century; from there it spread to the rest of Europe. The end of the fifteenth century saw a change in the rules which would be recognized by the modern player because the queen and bishop are allowed to move further around the board.

The first modern chess star was François-André Philidor, a Frenchman who, in 1749, added to the understanding of the game by writing a book about how to improve your game.

In 1886, the first world championship took place, and the first-ever world champion was Wilhelm Steinitz. The loser, Johannes Zukertort, came up with the unusual excuse that he performed badly due to the weather! At this time, the English player Howard Staunton lent his name to a design of chessman created by Nathaniel Cook. The Staunton chess set is now recognized as the standard and has sold more than one billion copies.

In the 1930s, the USA won most of the team tournaments until the Soviet Union decided to pour enormous amounts of money into chess. In 1948 a player named Mikhail Botvinnik won the world championship and the Soviets dominated all tournaments.

In 1985 Garry Kasparov became the youngest ever world champion and dominated chess for the next fifteen years. He made headlines around the world in 1997, when he lost to the computer Deep Blue. In a rematch five years later against the improved computer, Deep Junior, he drew a match to regain the respect of the chess world.

Today, the world chess federation, known as the Federation Internationale Des Echecs (FIDE) has over 100 countries as members, and millions of people play the game for fun.

# CHESS TIMELINE

| | |
|---|---|
| **A.D. 500** | Chaturanga, an early version of chess, is played in India. |
| **A.D. 600** | Chess is mentioned in Persion literature, where a hero is noted as a skillful horse rider and chess player. |
| **A.D. 1000** | Chess spreads to Spain, and other countries in Europe. |
| **1475** | The modern laws of chess are introduced. |
| **1851** | The first international chess tournament is held in London, England, and uses the Staunton chess set for the first time. |
| **1886** | Wilhelm Steinitz becomes the first official world champion. |
| **1930s** | The USA wins most team tournaments. |
| **1948** | The Soviet Union begins to dominate chess. |
| **1997** | World champion Garry Kasparov loses to a chess computer, Deep Blue. |
| **2003** | Garry Kasparov tries to have revenge for mankind, but only draws a match 3-3 against the computer known as Deep Junior. |
| **2004** | Vladimir Kramnik wins the biggest tournament of the year at Linares, Spain. Garry Kasparov is second, after winning only one game and drawing the rest. |

**AMAZING FACT** At Brighton Chess Club in England during the 1930s, a Mrs. Sydney was allowed to bring along her dog – but only if her dog joined the club! Later the dog, called Mr. Mick, was mistakenly picked for the club's second team. He lost for taking too much time.

**AMAZING FACT** The first chess book was printed in England, in 1475. It was called "The Game and Playe of the Chesse."

# FIRST LESSONS

Let's get started on learning to play chess! Chess is a game for two players. The aim of the game is to trap the other player's king. This is called the checkmate. The idea is to capture pieces and remove them from the board, as a way to help you checkmate. The player you are playing is called your opponent. Sometimes, you may even think of him/her as the enemy!

## THE BOARD

This is how the board and pieces should look, before a game begins. Each person has 16 pieces on a board of 64 squares. White always makes the first move. If the colors of the pieces are something strange, such as red and yellow, then the lighter color will start first.

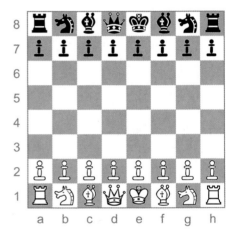

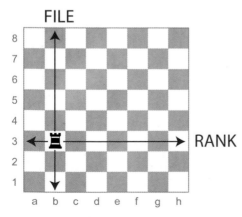

A good way to make sure the board is the right way round is to remember that there is always a white square on the right hand side – so it is "white in the right." "Rank" is a row of squares across the board and "file" is a vertical row of squares, running down the board.

# THE ROOK

Each player has two rooks at the start of the game. The rook moves forwards, backwards or to either side, in a straight line. It cannot jump pieces, except when making a special move called "castling," which is shown later on Page 18, when the rook can jump over the king.

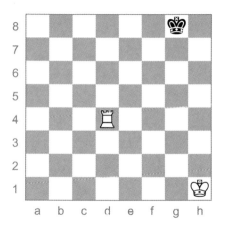

**AMAZING FACT** The rook looks like a tower from a medieval castle, so it is sometimes known as "the castle."

## Taking a Piece

The white rook can capture the black rook by moving in a straight line up the board, removing it from the board and occupying the square. A good way to know when to take a piece is to know how much it is worth. A rook is worth 5 points.

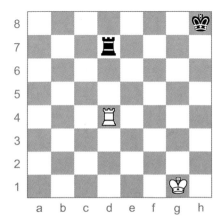

# THE KNIGHT

Each player has two knights at the start of the game. The knight is the only piece that jumps every move. It can hop over its own pieces or the opponent's pieces, by moving two squares in one direction, and then one square either side, as shown in the diagram at the bottom. It can move forwards, sideways and backwards. An easy way to remember how to move the knight is to think of an L shape.

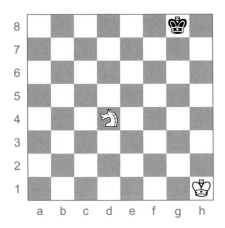

## Taking a Piece

The knight shown here can capture the rook, remove it from the board and occupy the square. The knight is worth 3 points.

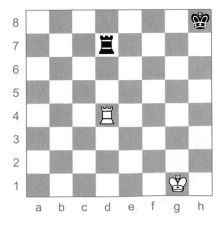

**10**

# THE BISHOP

Each player has two bishops at the start of the game. A bishop moves across the board, along the diagonal, backwards or forwards. If it starts the game on a black square, it moves only along those squares during the game. The other bishop will cover the white squares.

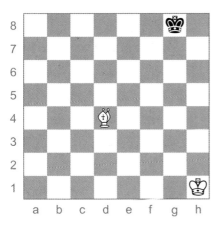

## Taking a Piece

The bishop shown here can move backwards, capture the knight, remove it from the board and occupy the square. The bishop is worth 3 points.

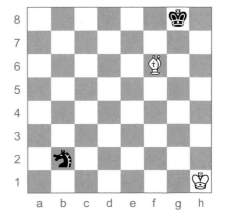

# THE QUEEN

Each player has one queen at the start of the game. The queen is the most powerful piece on the board. It can move in any direction, diagonally, forwards, backwards, or either side, but it cannot jump pieces.

## Taking a Piece

The queen shown here can move sideways, capture the bishop, remove it from the board and occupy the square. The queen is worth 9 points.

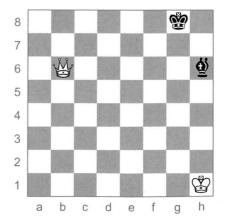

**TIP!** At the start of the game, the white queen should always be on a light square and the black queen should always be on a dark square.

# THE PAWN

Each player has eight pawns at the start of the game. The pawn usually moves forward one square at a time. However, on its first move, it has the option of moving two squares forward. It cannot move backwards or sideways.

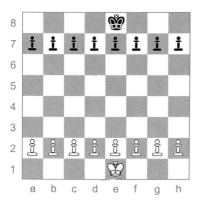

## Taking a Piece

Pawns are strange in that they capture pieces by moving diagonally one square. Pawns cannot take a piece by moving forward. The pawn shown here can capture the knight, remove it from the board and occupy the square. The pawn is worth 1 point.

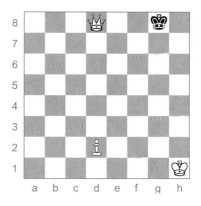

## Promotion

After a pawn reaches the eighth square, then a queen from another chess set can be used, or an upside-down rook. It is possible to have more than one queen on your side.

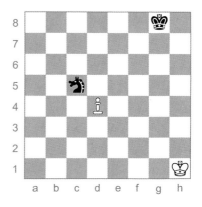

# THE KING

Each player has one king at the start of each game. The king is the most important piece on the board because if it is threatened, and cannot avoid the threat of being taken, then it is in checkmate and you lose the game. Just remember that the king is never removed from the board.

The king is a slow piece, moving one square at a time in any direction, although it can be safely guarded by a special move called "castling," which is shown on Page 18.

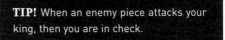

**TIP!** When an enemy piece attacks your king, then you are in check.

## Taking a Piece
The king shown here takes the pawn, removes it from the board and then occupies the square the pawn was on.

# CHECKMATE

The object of the game of chess is to trap your opponent's king. Checkmate is simply when the king is under attack and cannot escape. It is not possible to capture the opposing king and remove it from the board. Instead, checkmate is announced and the game is finished!

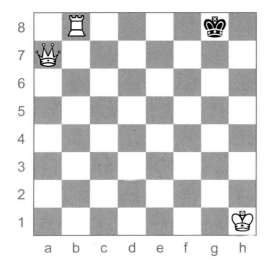

In the game shown here, the white rook attacks the king and the king cannot move up a square, because the queen covers all the squares on the seventh rank (remember, the rank is the row of squares running across the board).

## Resignation
When a player has a very bad position, or is about to be checkmated, he or she can resign to finish the game. Resignation happens when the loser knocks over their own king, to show he or she wants to stop.

## Check
When a player attacks an opponent's king by threatening to take it, but the king can escape, it is check. The game continues after the king escapes.

# TAKING PIECES

The game of chess is won with checkmate, but you can help to do that by taking as many enemy pieces as possible. A good way to know when to take a piece is to remember how many points each piece is worth.

PAWN = 1 point

BISHOP = 3 points

KNIGHT = 3 points

ROOK = 5 points

QUEEN = 9 points

KING = Safety is important. If checkmate occurs, the game is over!

## The Fork

When two pieces are attacked at the same time, it is called a fork. In the position shown here, the white knight has the black king in check. It is also a threat to the black queen. The king must move. This allows the white knight to take the queen.

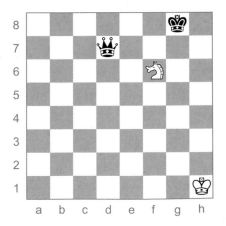

**AMAZING FACT** The slowest chess player ever was Louis Paulsen, who once thought for eleven hours over one move!

# Thinking Carefully

It is important to always think carefully before taking a piece. For example, if the white bishop shown here moves forward along the diagonal and takes the pawn, it is not a good idea. This is because the black king can then take the bishop (3 points), while white has only won a pawn (1 point).

When a player is considering taking a piece, they should look carefully at all of their opponent's pieces, to ensure they aren't making a mistake!

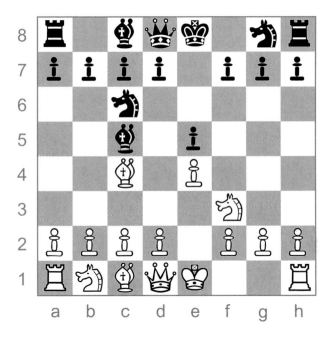

"**Chess is a cold bath for the mind.**" – Andrew Bonar Law, Former Prime Minister of Britain

# CASTLING

It is possible to move your king to safety with a special move called castling. Castling can only be done if there are no pieces between the rook and the king.

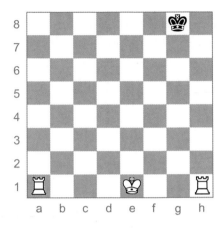

Here the king moves two squares sideways to the right, and puts the rook beside it. This is called kingside castling, because it is on the side of the board where the king started the game.

Here the king moves two squares sideways to the left, and puts the rook beside it. This is called queenside castling, because it is on the side of the board where the queen started the game.

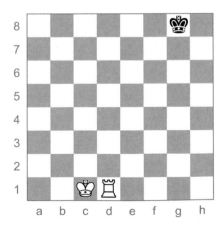

**TIP!** Each player can only castle once in a game. If the king or rook has already moved, then you are not allowed to castle.

# A SPECIAL MOVE

If you want to play a good game of chess, all you have to do is learn to move the pieces well. When you become more experienced at the game, you have to know a special move called "en passant," which means "in passing," in French. This expression is understood by chess players around the world, and is a rule to stop a pawn advancing two squares and sneaking past an enemy pawn.

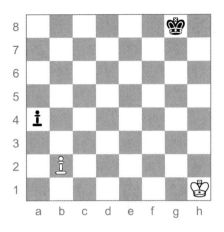

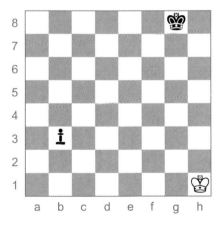

If the white pawn advances two squares, then the black pawn has the option of taking "en passant." The black pawn captures diagonally and is on the third rank (line across the board), as if the white pawn had only advanced one square, and had then been taken. This move is very useful to know.

---

**AMAZING FACT** The Australian Cecil Purdy was the first person to win the World Correspondence Championship, in 1953. Every move had to be sent by post to a player living in a different country. The longest game took three years!

---

"Chess is life in miniature. Chess is struggle, chess is battles." – Garry Kasparov, former World Chess Champion

# HOW TO DRAW

A good chess game might end in a draw, if the players are equally brilliant and agree to stop the game by one saying "draw" and the other accepting by shaking hands. This is something that top players might do after thinking for hours, so it's not a good idea for less experienced players, who want to learn to be better at the game.

## Draw Number One – Stalemate

This is an example of a stalemate. It is White's turn to play and he or she cannot move any pawns or pieces. The king is not in check but is unable to move. It is important to know that two kings cannot move next to each other, and you cannot put your king into check. The game is drawn. In tournaments, you receive one point for a win and half a point for a draw.

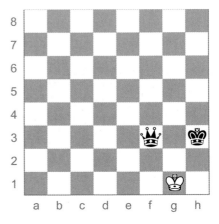

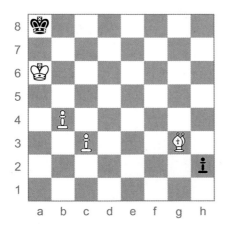

In this position, from an Australian tournament, the black player has been losing the game but finally sees a chance. He advances his pawn and wants to promote a queen. White has to take the pawn, and it is stalemate because the black king cannot make a move.

## Draw Number Two – Repeating Moves

If a position is repeated three times, then the game is drawn. It usually occurs when one side can keep checking and there is no way out.

In this example, White cannot take the black queen or block the check, so the king has to move. The black queen checks the white king by moving one square sideways. There is no escape, so Black can keep checking and the position is repeated three times.

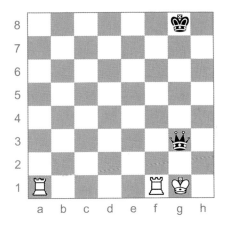

## Draw Number Three – The Boring Draw

This draw occurs when no pawns have been moved, or no captures have taken place for fifty moves. It hardly ever happens!

**AMAZING FACT** The longest game ever in a world championship game is 124 moves, between Victor Korchnoi and Anatoly Karpov in 1978. The game ended in a stalemate.

"Chess is a sea in which a gnat may drink and an elephant may bathe."

– Indian proverb

# WRITING CHESS MOVES

When you are playing chess it is a good idea to write down your chess moves.
• You can keep all your best games forever.
Why do people write down chess moves and read moves from other games?
• You can read other chess games in newspapers and books, and learn from them.

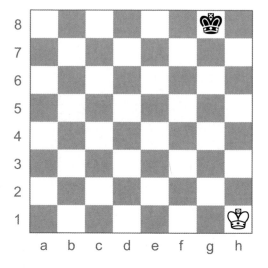

The code for writing down chess moves is called algebraic notation. It uses numbers and letters on the side of the board, to make it easy. It may take a little while to learn how to write down chess moves, but it is important to do so.

The chess pieces all have special letters, except for the pawn. A move can be written by using the letter for the pieces you are moving, and then which square you have moved it to, using the letter and numbers on the side of the board.

**Rook = R**

**Queen = Q**

**Bishop = B**

**King = K**

**Knight = N (to avoid mistakes because the king is already called K)**

**The pawn has no letter.**

## NOTATION CORNER

| | |
|---|---|
| **Check:** | **+** at the end of the move. For example, **Re1+** |
| **Checkmate:** | **++** at the end of the move. For example, **Qxf7++**. |
| **Castling:** | **0-0** is when you castle on the kingside. **0-0-0** is when you castle on the queenside. |
| **Promotion:** | **c8 Q** is when a c-pawn is on the eighth square and promotes to a queen. |
| **Taking a piece:** | When a rook takes a bishop on a8 the move is **Rxa8**. A sign that something has been taken is shown by **x**. |
| **Mistake:** | **?** after a move indicates a mistake, but should only be written after the game has finished. |
| **The final score:** | A white win is shown by **1-0**, a black win is shown by **0-1** and [ **-** ] shows a draw. |

## Example

White to play 1 **axb4** or 1 **Qxa7** or
1 **0-0-0** or 1 **0-0** or 1 **h4**.
Black to play 1 ... **Nxc2+** or 1 ... **Bxh3**.

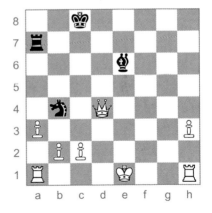

## Puzzle 1

Black to play and checkmate in one move. How do you write the move?
*Answer on Page 47.*

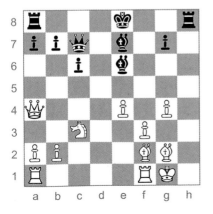

# YOUR FIRST GAME

## Scholar's Mate

Here is an example of a short game. You may like to set a chessboard up and try out this game. White always moves first.

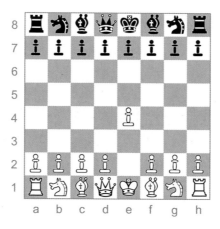

**1 e4**

The pawn is advanced two squares, which will allow the queen and the white bishop to move.

**1 . . . e5**

Black plays the same as White, so that his queen and black bishop can move.

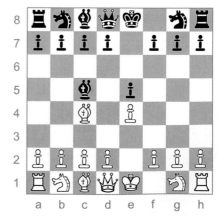

**2 Bc4**

The bishop moves out.

**2 . . . Bc5**

Black copies White by moving the bishop out.

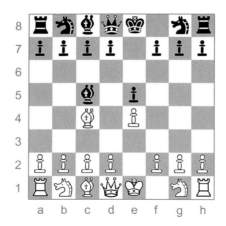

### 3 Qf3

The white queen joins in the action and targets the f7 pawn, which is also attacked by the bishop.

### 3 ... Nc6?

Black makes a mistake and does not spot White's threat.

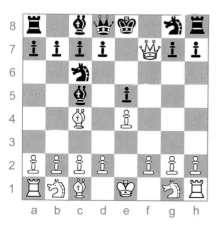

### 4 Qxf7++ checkmate 1-0

White wins the game and this checkmate in four moves is known as Scholar's Mate.

Remember, it is polite to shake hands after the game!

## Chess Clocks

In tournaments, players use a special chess clock which has two clock faces. After making a move, a player presses their side of the clock, which starts the time of their opponent and stops their own. A game can be as little as five minutes each, or as long as several hours.

# CHESS OPENINGS FOR WHITE

The first ten moves for each side are known as the opening moves in a game of chess. The player with the white pieces has a small advantage because they start first. They can decide what kind of game will occur, such as an attacking or defensive game. It is a bit like tennis, when the person who serves can try to force their opponent to defend.

Here are some rules to help you:

## Move the Pawns to the Center

This opening is good for White, because the pawns help to control the middle of the board. It is also possible for the bishops and queen to move. In this game, black has started badly because the advance of the a-pawn only allows **Ra6**, but then the white bishop could take it.

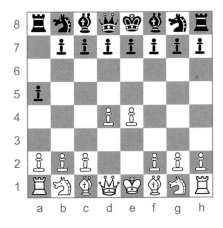

**TIP!** Copy the stars to learn an opening. Look at Garry Kasparov's games and you will soon learn how to start the game.

## Move the Pieces

The more pieces that you move, the more chances there are to win pieces, or checkmate.

**1 e4, e5  2 Nf3, Nc6  3 Bc4, Bc5**

This is an example of an opening known as Giuoco Piano (quiet game), named by the Italians in medieval days. Both sides have good chances to win.

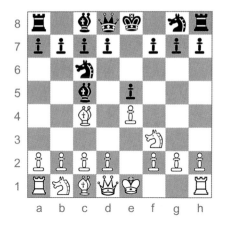

## Make a Threat

It is a good idea to make threats to win pieces, or play checkmate because your opponent might not.

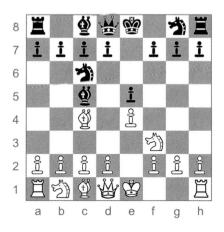

**1 e4, e5  2 Nf3, d6  3 Bc4, f6?  4 d4, Ne7  5 dxe5, dxe5  6 Bf7+**

In the example shown here, White has checked the king after only six moves, and will win the black queen. Now the king cannot go on to the d-file because the white queen covers it. So he must take the bishop. The game continues **6 . . . Kxf7 7 Qxd8** and White is winning.

## Look After Your Pieces

**1 d4, d5  2 Nf3, Bg4  3 e3**

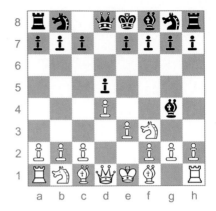

In this position from the Colle opening, White should be in no danger. If
Black takes the knight (3 points) with
his bishop (3 points), then the position
is level. This is because White can take
back the bishop and no points have
been lost.

For example: **3 . . . Bxf3 4 Qxf3.**

Remember that points are only useful as a guide to who is better, because you
can still be 10 points or more down and still play checkmate!

## Castle Your King

It is a good idea not to leave your king in the center where it can be attacked,
so you should castle in the opening.

**1 d4, d5  2 Nf3, Nf6  3 Bf4, e6  4 e3, Be7
5 Bd3, 0-0  6 0-0**

In the position shown here, from an
opening called the London System,
both sides have castled. The king is
safer, and it also means the king's rook
will be more useful than being stuck in
the corner.

**TIP!** Set up a chess board and prac-
tice each of the opening moves
shown for both White and Black.

# CHESS OPENINGS FOR BLACK

## Fool's Mate

**1 f3, e5   2 g4, Qh4++**

In this example, it is possible for White to lose after only two moves! It is checkmate because White cannot block or avoid the check, and Black has won the game. This two move checkmate is the quickest possible in chess and is known as Fool's Mate.

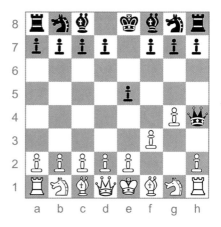

**TIP!** In the opening of a game, move your pieces out quickly and castle early.

# French Defense

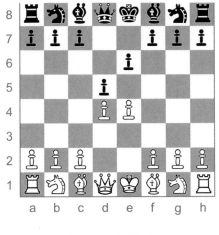

**1 e4, e6  2 d4, d5**

The moves in this example are a sign that Black is playing the French Defense. The advance of the black d-pawn allows the queen and bishop to move, and challenge White's pawn center. The main benefit of this strategy is that Black can play their favorite opening and it also avoids Scholar's Mate, the short game we showed you on Page 24. The position offers equal chances.

**TIP!** Consider the person you are playing, before deciding on an opening move. Are they an experienced player? Have they been playing chess longer than you? Will they see what opening move you are planning to use, or will you have the advantage? Chess is a game of strategy, so think carefully before you move!

**Top 10 Strange Opening Names**

1. Frankenstein-Dracula Variation
2. The Dragon
3. Bird's Opening
4. The St. George
5. The Clarendon Court
6. The Barry Attack
7. The Grand Prix Attack
8. The Orangutan
9. The Siesta Variation
10. Fried Liver Attack

# The Sicilian Defense

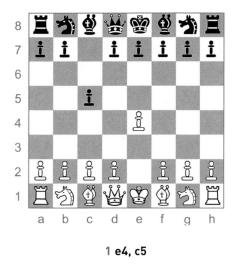

**1 e4, c5**

In this defense, Black plays the Sicilian, which is one of the most popular openings. The pawn advance allows the queen to move, and it covers d4 to stop White having strong pawns in the center. It is a good opening and one of Garry Kasparov's favorites.

# Queen's Gambit Declined

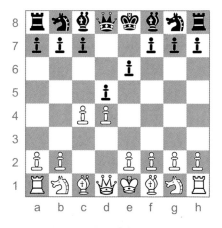

**1 d4, d5  2 c4, e6**

The moves shown here are a sign that Black is playing the Queen's Gambit Declined. The pawn on d5 is supported, and if White takes the pawn, then Black will take back with the e-pawn. A good, solid opening defense.

**TIP!** Always try to play on until checkmate and do not resign, even if your game is not going well. Remember, your opponent might make a mistake.

# ATTACKING CHESS

When playing attacking moves in chess, the player is not under immediate threat and is attempting to take their opponent's pieces. Here are two examples.

## The Pin

This is a good trick to know, and it happens when the piece really being threatened is behind a less valuable piece.

The black queen cannot move off the e-file because that would put the black king in check, which is not allowed. It means the queen is pinned, so the rook (5 points) can take the queen (9 points), and White is in a better position.

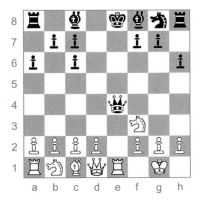

For keen players, this position happened after:
**1 e4, e5  2 Nf3, Nc6  3 Bb5, a6  4 Bxc6, dxc6  5 0-0, h6  6 Nxe5, Qd4  7 Nf3, Qxe4  8 Re1**

## The Skewer

This is like a pin, but it wins a piece by threatening a more important piece in front of it.

The black king shown here is in check, so it must move when White can take the black queen.

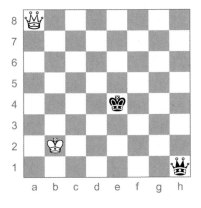

## Puzzle 2

White to play and win a piece. Can you see how?
*Answer on Page 47.*

# HOW TO DEFEND

It is fun to attack when playing chess, but sometimes your opponent attacks you! Then there is a need to defend.

In this position, white can defend with **Re5-e1**, and should win. This game was actually lost by White, after **1 Rxd1**, **Rxd1+** **2 Re1**, **Rxe1++** checkmate. This shows the need to know how to defend.

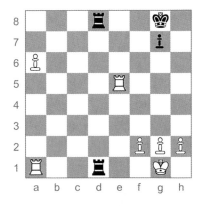

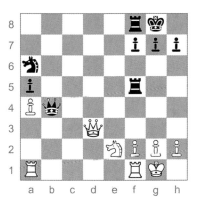

In this position after **1 e4, e5 2 Qh5** now **2 . . . Nc6** is a good idea to defend the e5 pawn. Not **2 . . . g6?** When **3 Qxe5+** is a skewer, because the king is in check and at the same time, the rook on h8 is attacked.

> **TIP!** If your piece is attacked, move or defend it.

## Do Not Lose Pieces

It is always a good idea to carefully defend your pieces, so they cannot be taken for free.

The white queen in this example is attacking the knight on a6, and the rook on f5. Black can defend with **1 . . . Rf6** when White will not want to take the knight, because it will be captured by the rook.

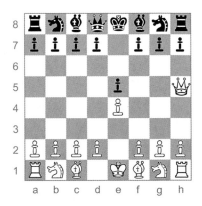

# THE MIDDLEGAME

The middlegame is the name given to the position in a chess game after the opening. This is the time to plan an attack on the enemy king, or try to win pieces.

Here are some things you should think about when you have to make a move:

1. Can I threaten checkmate?
2. Can I threaten a piece?
3. Can I move my pieces to better squares?
4. Is my king defended?
5. Are my pieces defended?

In this game, it is Black to move and the bishop on h6 cannot be taken by the pawn, because of the pin on the g-file by the white queen. White wants to take the g7 pawn with the queen and announce checkmate. This is because the black king would be threatened, cannot escape and cannot take the queen, which is defended. The only way to stop checkmate is **1 . . . g6** which allows **2 Bxf8**. Winning a piece for White.

## How To Win

There are times when you have to defend and there are times when you have to attack. In this case, with White to move, it seems that the worry is the black a-pawn advancing. In fact, White plays **1 Qf8+, Kxf8  2 Rd8++ checkmate**.

"**Chess is a sport.**" – Graeme Gardiner, former Australian Chess President

# TRICKS AND TRAPS

Here are some important tricks and traps for you to learn.

## Discovered Attack

In this position, Black can play **1 . . . Bxh2+** revealing a hidden attack on the white queen, so **2 Kxh2** is met by **2 . . . Qxd2** winning the white queen.

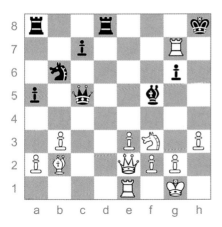

## Discovered Check

This is similar to Discovered Attack, because a piece is moved to reveal a hidden check. In this case, White can win pieces with **1 Rxc7+** revealing a hidden check, and at the same time, attacking the black queen.

## Puzzle 3

White to play and win an important piece.

*Answer on Page 47.*

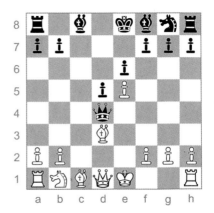

## Beating The Guard

The knight is guarding the pawn on h7 from attack, so White removes it from the board. **1 Bxf6, Qxf6** allows **2 Qxh7++ checkmate**.

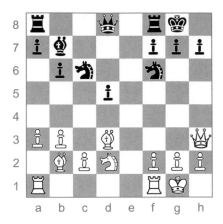

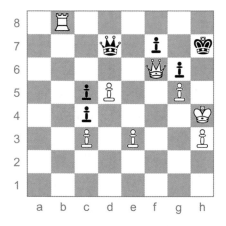

## Draw!

In the game shown here, it seems that Black is lost because of the checkmate threats and because of White's extra rook. Black now plays the amazing **1 . . . Qxh3+** and after **2 Kxh3** the position is stalemate! The black king cannot move without it being in check, and none of the black pawns can move.

**TIP!** Learn from your mistakes with every game of chess you play, and you will find you quickly improve as a player. You can also learn from your opponent's mistakes. Every so often, go over notations you've made from previous games to remind yourself of what to do the next time you play.

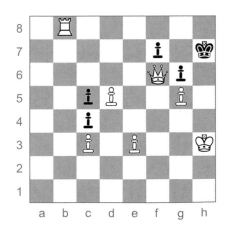

**AMAZING FACT** In the 1903 Monte Carlo tournament, Colonel Moreau had a record result. He lost all 26 games.

# THE ENDGAME

The game of chess has three parts:

**The Opening** – the first ten moves of the game.

**The Middlegame** – the part of the game when plans are decided and checkmate is threatened.

**The Endgame** – the final part of the game, when queens are exchanged. Also known simply as the ending.

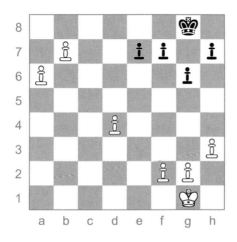

In this example, the white pawns on a6 and b7 will soon promote to queens, and White will win. It is often a good plan to try and promote a pawn in the endgame.

## Extra Piece

An extra piece in the endgame is very good news! It can be used to take the enemy pawns. Then a good plan would be to prepare checkmate, or try to promote one of your own pawns.

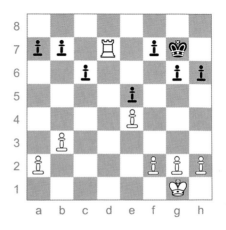

**TIP!** Be extra patient during the endgame and look carefully for possible chances to checkmate, before you move.

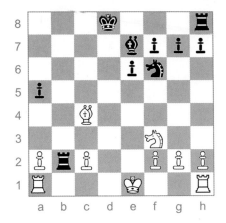

## Trap

In this game, White has just allowed a pawn to be taken on b2, but now plays
**1 0-0-0+**.

The black king must take evasive action, and the next move, White can play
**2 Kxb2**, winning the black rook.

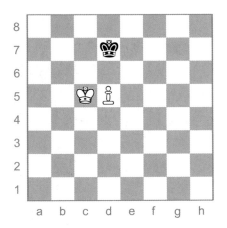

## Draw

This example shows a basic position in the endgame, but an important one. It is a draw with correct play, but Black has to be careful. **1 d6, Kd8** (**1 . . . Kc8** loses after **2 Kc6, Kd8 3 d7 Ke7, 4 Kc7** and the white pawn will queen) **2 Kc6, Kc8 3 d7+, Kd8 4 Kd6 stalemate**.

**TIP!** Always try to play on until checkmate and do not resign, even if your game is not going well. Remember, your opponent might make a mistake.

"In chess, knowing what to do is half the battle; knowing when to do it is the other half."- Anon

# EXTRA CHECKMATE

There are lots of chances to checkmate in the endgame, and when playing you must plan ahead and look out for them.

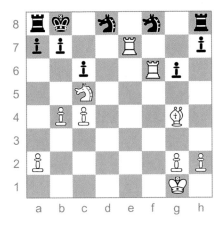

Here White can play **1 Rxb7+** Followed by **1 . . . Nxb7 2 Na6++ checkmate**.

## Checkmate with Rooks

In this example, the black king is under attack and cannot avoid check. It is checkmate and White has won the game!

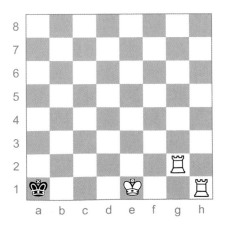

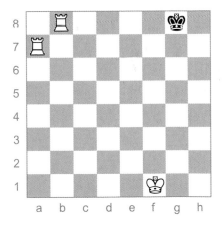

## Puzzle 4

Can you spot how White can checkmate in one move?

*Answer on Page 47.*

# CHESS AND COMPUTERS

Chess is a game that has been played for more than 1,500 years, but it wasn't until the twentieth century that machines that could truly play the game were invented.

The first chess-playing machine ever invented turned out to be a fake. Known as The Turk, it became very famous after it was first shown to Empress Maria Theresa of Austria, in 1769. The mechanical device amazed spectators for some time and even beat Emperor Napoleon of France, in 1809. The mystery of how it worked was solved many years later, when it was revealed that a secret compartment in the large machine hid a man who really played the moves!

The history of computers and chess is closely linked, because programmers believed that if they could design a machine that played well at chess, then anything was possible. In 1950, Claude Shannon, a scientist at Bell Laboratories in the USA, published an article discussing chess computers. It proved to be an inspiration, and encouraged many other scientists to work on developing chess computers.

In 1957, artificial intelligence pioneers Herbert Simon and Allen Newell predicted a human would lose to a computer within ten years. Therefore, there was great excitement in 1958 when the first computer to play chess, an IBM 704, was built. Unfortunately, it was hopeless at the game. The only way for a computer to beat someone in those days was if the human was someone who barely knew how to move the pieces.

Chess computers first became available in the shops, in 1976. Even then, they still played rather badly. Since that time, enormous improvements have been made and anyone can now buy a program that is good enough to compete with a master.

The chess battle between mankind and computers really hit the headlines in 1997.

World Number One, Garry Kasparov, sensationally lost a match against a chess program running on a high-powered computer called Deep Blue (mentioned briefly earlier in this book). Kasparov called it "The silicon monster." Deep Blue was estimated to be able to analyze two million positions per second.

A human quickly selects the best possibilities and will not consider silly moves, such as losing the queen, but a computer tries to look at everything. Kasparov tried to seek revenge in 2003 when he took on the powerful program, Deep Junior, but he narrowly failed in his challenge and the match ended in a draw.

## How to Beat Your Computer

The best advice we can give, is that each time you are losing, shut the computer down! It has to be admitted that chess programs for personal computers are getting stronger and stronger. This is a good thing, because it is possible to use them as a teaching device. Also, by changing the level of play, you always have a chance of winning. And your opponent never gets bored.

There are some chess games on the market today with amazing graphics. You can play regular chess, or watch as exciting action unfolds on the screen in front of you after each move, showing battles between the different chess pieces. Handsome knights and kings, beautiful queens, stately bishops, towering rooks and lowly pawns. Don't let these incredible graphics distract you from your main aim – winning the game!

## A Chess Club That Never Closes

There is a place where you can play chess twenty-four hours a day, every day of the year. It is called the Internet! There are lots of sites where you can play people of your own level, and even watch the stars battling it out in cyberspace.

It is possible to play quick games such as five minutes each person, and there are even games with one minute time limits. Of course, it is also possible to find players who would like a longer game.

# A FAMOUS GAME

Here is a famous game that took place many years ago, and is still remembered by chess players today as one of the best!

## Edward Lasker – Sir George Thomas.
## London, England, 1912

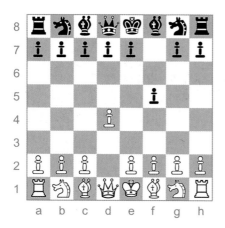

**1 d4, f5**
The opening by Black is known as the Dutch Defense.

**2 e4** The pawn is offered to Black and this is known as a gambit. If Black takes the gambit pawn, then White will try to move his pieces out quickly, and will attempt to take the pawn back.
**2 . . . fxe4 3 Nc3, Nf6 4 Bg5, e6 5 Nxe4, Be7 6 Bxf6, Bxf6 7 Nf3, 0-0**

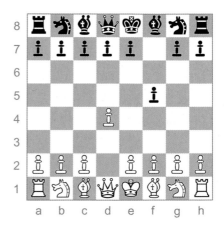

Black castles early, which is normally a good idea. But now White will try to attack the black king.

This incredible game continued...

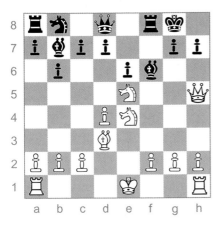

**8 Bd3, b6 9 Ne5, Bb7 10 Qh5**

White moves the queen into the attack.

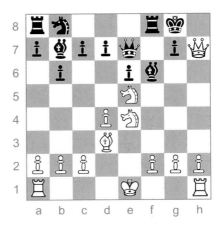

The threat is **11 Nxf6+, gxf6 12 Qxh7++**
checkmate. **10 . . . Qe7 11 Qxh7+**

A fantastic move, which sacrifices a
queen for a brilliant attack.

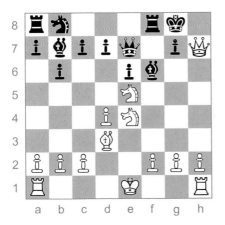

**11 . . . Kxh7 12 Nxf6+, Kh6**
The king has to move to h6 because it
was double-check, and if it had moved
backward to h8 White could have
caught him in a fork.
**13 Neg4+, Kg5**

Tension built, as the endgame progressed

**"When the chess game is over, the pawn and the king go back to the
same box."** - Irish saying

**14 h4+**

The king is being chased up the board. In fact, many years after the game was played, it was discovered that there was a quicker way to win after **14 f4+, Kxf4 (or 14 ... Kh4 15 g3+, Kh3 16 Bf1+, Bg2 17 Nf2++ checkmate) 15 g3+, Kf3 16 0-0++ checkmate**.

Instead the game progressed like this **14 ... Kf4  15 g3+, Kf3  16 Be2+, Kg2 17 Rh2+, Kg1**

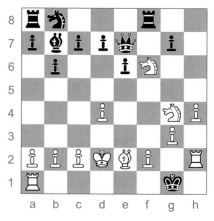

And finally...
**18 Kd2++ checkmate 1-0**

Well done if you also saw that **18 0-0-0++** is checkmate.

# Puzzle 5

Gary Lane – Ian Rogers, Gold Coast, Australia, 2001.

White to play checkmate in three moves.
*Answer on Page 47.*

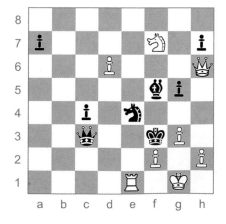

# GLOSSARY

**attack** a strategy played when the player is not under threat, and is attempting to capture the opponent's chess pieces

**capture** when a piece is taken

**castling** a king moves two squares sideways and the rook jumps over the king

**checkmate** the king is being attacked, so it is in check and cannot escape

**defense** a strategy aimed at protecting your chess pieces from an opponent's attack

**development** the pieces are moved from their original squares

**endgame** the queens have been exchanged and normally, there are few pieces left on the board

**en passant** a special move, which allows an advanced enemy pawn to take a pawn that has just moved two squares, as though it had moved one square forward

**fork** a row of squares running down the board

**king's side** one piece attacks two pieces at the same time the side of the board on which the king starts the game

**middlegame** the middle part of the game, after the opening, where plans are usually made to attack or defend

**notation** the code for writing chess moves is algebraic notation

**opening** the first part of the game – the first ten moves

**opponent** the name given to the person you are playing against

**pin** a piece is attacked, and if it moves, a more valuable piece will be taken

**perpetual check** a player repeatedly puts the other player in check, and with no escape, it is a draw

**queen's side** the side of the board where the queen starts the game

**rank** a row of squares running across the board

**sacrifice** when a chess piece is given up, to help the attack or defense

**skewer** a valuable piece is attacked and if it moves, a less valuable piece can be taken

**stalemate** a position when the king is not in check, but has no possible move by any piece, ending the game in a draw

**touch move** if you touch a piece and it is your move, then you have to move it

# MOVING ON

A good way to improve your chess skills is to play lots of games. If you are playing against someone slightly better than you, then you will quickly improve. Of course, if that is not possible you could go on the Internet and challenge someone from anywhere in the world!

## Books
There are many chess books available to help improve your game. Check your favorite bookstore or local library for available titles.

## Computer Software
Chess software for the computer is also a useful way to test your skills, but remember to change the level of standard to suit your play.

## Useful Websites
You will find a limitless number of useful websites as well as Chess Federations simply by putting the word "chess" in your search engine. Among the leading Chess Federations in the world are The USA Chess Federation, The Australian Chess Federation, the British Chess federation, the New Zealand Chess Federation and the Canadian Chess Federation.

# PUZZLE ANSWERS

## Puzzle 1
Runicamon-Lane, Noosa, Australia, 2002. The game finished with **1 . . . Qh2++ checkmate**.

## Puzzle 2
1 Ra8 The black queen is attacked and when it moves, White can play **2 Rxe8+** winning a piece.

## Puzzle 3
**1 Bb5+** reveals a hidden attack against the black queen, and after Black moves, the white Queen can play **2 Qxd4**.

## Puzzle 4
**1 0-0++** is checkmate.

## Puzzle 5
The game finished with **1 Ne5+, Qxe5 2 Re3+, Kg4 3 h3++ checkmate**. Well done if you also saw **1 Qh5+, Bg4 2 Ne5+, Qxe5 3 Re3++ checkmate**.

# ABOUT THE AUTHOR

**Gary Lane** learned to play chess at the age of eight with the help of his brother, Nigel, who gave up soon after he started losing! Gary is an international chess master and has been a professional chess player in Europe. He played for club teams in countries such as Belgium, France, England, Germany and Holland. Since winning the Commonwealth Championship he has established himself as a prominent figure on the tournament circuit.

Gary is a renowned chess trainer, and has been involved in coaching some of England and Australia's top junior players. He now lives in Sydney, Australia, and is the current Australian Chess Champion.